BEFORE YOU BEGIN...

Make sure to download the FREE audio program for this book which comes with your purchase! Just go to

www.slangman.com/audio

then look for your book and enter this code:

E2I3ZHMC42C5

Beauty and the Beast

Written by: David Burke
Copy Editor: Julie Bobrick
Illustrated by: "Migs!" Sandoval
Translator: Alessio Filippi
Proofreader: Valerio Morucci

Copyright © 2017 by David Burke

Email: info@heywordy.com
Website: www.heywordy.com

Hey Wordy! and all related characters and elements are © and trademarks of Hey Wordy, LLC.

Published by Slangman Publishing. Slangman is a registered trademark of David Burke. All rights reserved. Reproduction or translation of any part of this work beyond that permitted by section 107 or 108 of the 1976 United States Copyright Act without the permission of the copyright owner is unlawful. Requests for permission or further information should be addressed to the Permissions Department, Slangman Publishing. This publication is designed to provide accurate and authoritative information in regard to the subject matter covered. The persons, entities and events in this book are fictitious. Any similarities with actual persons or entities, past and present, are purely coincidental.

ISBN13: 978-1-891888-49-6

Printed in the U.S.A.

Meet the Author
David Burke

Creator and star of the children's TV show, *Hey Wordy!*, David Burke has been single-handedly revolutionizing the foreign language-learning movement worldwide.

In addition to being a performer of boundless energy and enthusiasm, David speaks seven languages. A successful author and entrepreneur, he has built a thriving international publishing company featuring over 100 books he has written for teen/adults & children. His books have won publishing awards and have sold more than one million copies. David's Street Speak™ and Biz Speak™ series of books and audio programs are used around the world by government agencies, leading universities and major corporations.

Since age 4, David has been a classically trained pianist and uses his musical gifts to compose and perform original songs for his TV series, *Hey Wordy!* which introduces children to foreign languages and cultures through music, animation, and magical adventures. He has also composed, orchestrated, and performed all the music in the audio programs for each of these books.

David's engaging and charismatic persona became a fixture on broadcast entertainment channels around the world, such as CNN and the BBC. David and his work have been highlighted in many major publications, including The Los Angeles Times, The Chicago Tribune and The Christian Science Monitor.

"This series teaches everyday words that occur in your child's life, as well as terms having to do with politeness, greetings, family & friendship."

David Burke

Italian vocabulary taught:

anello = ring
bestia = beast
buon = good
brutta = ugly
buon giorno = hello
cavallo = horse
cinque = five
collana = necklace
figlia = daughter
gentile = kind
giardino = garden

mezzogiorno = noon
molto = very much
per favore = please
pranzo = lunch
quattro = four
regalo = gift
rosa = rose
sei = six
signore = sir
ti amo = I love you
viaggio = trip

One thing to remember...

The words in *green italics* throughout this fairy tale are words you've already learned in the previous level! Do you still remember what they mean?

from Cinderella (Level 1)

arrivederci = goodbye
bella = pretty
bello = handsome
casa = house
cattiva = mean
felice = happy
festa = party
grande = big
grazie = thank you
innamorato = in love

mezzanotte = midnight
moglie = wife
momento = moment
piede = foot
prego = you're welcome
principe = prince
ragazza = girl
scarpa = shoe
triste = sad
vestito = dress

from Goldilocks & The Three Bears (Level 2)

bambino = baby
caldo = hot
ciotola = bowl
cucina = kitchen
cuscino = cushion
due = two
duro = hard
freddo = cold
letto = bed
mamma = mama
morbido = soft

orso = bear
papà = papa
passeggiata = stroll
piccolo = little
poltrona = armchair
porta = door
stanca = tired
tavola = table
tre = three
uno = one

figlia

molto

Once upon a time, there was a *papà* who had an eldest (daughter) named Julie, a middle **figlia** named Tessa, and a youngest **figlia** named Bella. He loved them (very much). Before taking a long (trip), he asked each **figlia**, "What can I bring you from my **viaggio**?" "I'd like a (ring) to wear on my finger," said Julie. "I'd like a (necklace) to wear around my neck," said Tessa.

viaggio
anello
collana

Per favore — Please

rosa — rose

But Bella, who was the most **bella** of all said, "Please. I don't want an **anello** to wear on my finger or a **collana** to wear around my neck. All I want is a rose." He replied, "You shall each receive your gift." "Oh, *grazie! Grazie!*" said each **figlia**. Then their *papà* mounted his horse as they shouted "Have a good *viaggio, papà!* **Buon viaggio**! We will miss you **molto**!"

→ **regalo**
→ **cavallo**
→ **buon**

As he rode off, each **figlia** shouted again, "*Arrivederci, papà! Arrivederci!*" until he was out of sight. Days later, it was time for him to return. So he first stopped to buy an **anello**

for his eldest **figlia** to wear on her finger, a **collana** for his second **figlia** to wear around her neck, but he waited to get closer to his *casa* to look for a garden where he could

giardino

find a **rosa** for Bella. After a few hours, he saw a magnificent **giardino**. He got off his **cavallo**, walked into the **giardino** and picked a **bella rosa**. At that **momento**, the *porta* to the *casa* opened and a *grande* [beast] came out and ran toward him. "Who dares to steal a **rosa** from my **giardino**?" exploded the *grande* **bestia**. "**Per favore**,

bestia

9

signore ← [sir]!" said the *papà*. "Don't hurt me, **signore**. I promised my *figlia* that I'd bring her a **rosa** as a **regalo** after my long **viaggio**. It was just ONE **rosa** from your **giardino**!" "It's still stealing!" said the **grande bestia**. "I will spare your life if you bring me the **figlia** you speak of by noon in six days. Here she will live the rest of her life." Naturally,

→ **mezzogiorno**
→ **sei**

the **papà** was very **triste** by this request, but he promised to return with Bella at **mezzogiorno** in **sei** days. As he arrived home, each **figlia** rushed out to greet him. He gave them each the **regalo** they'd asked for. Each **figlia** was very *felice* and shouted, "*Grazie, papà. Grazie!*" "*Prego!*" he replied. But he was still *triste* because he had to tell Bella

13

ti amo

about the promise he'd made with the *grande bestia*. "Bella, I love you. **Ti amo molto**, and want you to be *felice*. But I must tell you what I have done…" Her *papà* went on to explain what had happened that day and about the promise he had made. He warned her about how ugly the *grande* **bestia** was, but Bella felt responsible because the **rosa** was a

brutta

regalo she'd requested. So she agreed to go. **Sei** days passed quickly and it was now the **momento** to leave. Each sister was very *triste* to say *arrivederci* to Bella but they understood that she had no choice. So, Bella and her *papà* mounted the **cavallo** and rode off. They arrived at exactly **mezzogiorno** as instructed. Bella and her *papà* got off the **cavallo** and approached the

Buon giorno

casa. The *porta* opened slowly and they walked in. "Hello!" said the *papà*. "**Buon giorno**!" But there was no answer. As they walked forward, they saw a *grande tavola* in the *cucina* filled with food. It looked like someone was having a *grande festa*! Just then they heard a deep voice say, "**Buon giorno**. This lunch is especially for you. **Per favore**, enjoy!" Not

pranzo

wanting to be impolite, they began eating the magnificent **pranzo** before them. And so many desserts! Bella was so excited and already busily counting all of them, "...four,

quattro

cinque

five , **sei**! **Sei** different desserts! She counted them again just to make sure, "*Uno*, *due*, *tre*, **quattro**, **cinque**, **sei**! It was true! **Sei** delicious desserts! They had never seen a more wonderful **pranzo** in their lives! Suddenly, there before them, appeared the **grande bestia** himself. Indeed, the **bestia** was truly **brutta**. Scared, Bella said, "**Buon giorno, Signore** and *grazie* for the **pranzo**." "*Prego*," replied the *grande* **bestia**. He seemed very kind toward Bella. Her *papà* was permitted to come visit her

gentile

every week which made her very *felice*. He gave Bella a kiss on the cheek, mounted his **cavallo**, and said, "*Arrivederci*, Bella. **Ti amo**, my **bella figlia**!" and rode off. At that *momento*, the **grande bestia** turned toward Bella and said, "**Per favore**. What's mine is yours. I will return every day at **mezzogiorno** to see you." He then quickly ran off, leaving

Bella alone. Because he was so **gentile** toward her, Bella was no longer afraid, and was even *felice* when he came to visit at **mezzogiorno**. Every day, they laughed more and more and enjoyed sharing stories with each other. But one day, the **grande bestia** didn't arrive at **mezzogiorno** as usual, so Bella went to look for him. She walked outside into the

giardino and there he was lying on the ground lifeless. Bella cried, "Oh, why did you have to die? **Ti amo**, *grande* **bestia**! **Ti amo molto**!" She leaned over and gave him a kiss on the cheek and suddenly, right before her eyes, he awoke and was transformed into a **principe** who was truly **bello**! He explained to her that an evil magician had changed him into a **grande bestia** and only the kiss from someone who was truly *innamorato* with him could change him back. The next day at **mezzogiorno**, Bella became his *moglie*, and they all lived happily ever after.

Now you're ready for Levels 4 & 5!

Levels 4 & 5 contain the words from Levels 1, 2 and 3 plus all NEW words!

For more HEY WORDY! products, visit...